more than ok.

a guide for anxiety&depression

joe & kristin jardine
daniel & rennié simpson

The Reset Group

 @theresetgroup

 @therealreset

 www.theresetgroup.com

 The Reset Group

You Flourishing

 @ youflourishing

 @youflourishing

 www.youflourishing.com

 @youflourishing

We are a group of licensed mental health professionals who work with top tier athletes, coaches, organizations, churches, and families to develop the winning mindset of leaders to overcome mental blocks in all areas of life.

Edited and Illustrated by Bryson Breakey
Updated 5.23.20

ARE YOU READY FOR A BREAKTHROUGH?
We do life coaching for individuals struggling with depression, anxiety, life transitions, and couples who are fighting for their marriage. Contact us for more information at www.theresetgroup.com/take-action

Speaking inquiries email us at joe@theresetgroup.com

table of contents.

WELCOME   11

RESET EMOTIONS   19
Day 1 name it and claim it   21
Day 2 where do you feel it?   25
Day 3 what worries you?   29
Day 4 let's get artsy   33
Day 5 grounded   35
Day 6 perspective shift   37
Day 7 fun   39
Day 8 foundation recap   41

RENEW MIND   45
Day 9 self-talk   47
Day 10 stinking thinking   49
Day 11 how our thoughts lie to us   53
Day 12 the "what-if" technique   57
Day 13 attitude of gratitude   61
Day 14 from monologue to dialogue   63
Day 15 small wins   65
Day 16 no more than three   67
Day 17 chaos to order   69
Day 18 what are your triggers   73
Day 19 trigger antidotes   77
Day 20 where the mind goes the body goes   81
Day 21 foundation recap   85

RESTORE SPIRIT   89
Day 22 prioritizing God   91
Day 23 drawing near to God   95
Day 24 write a psalm   97
Day 25 make a date with nature   101
Day 26 footloose   105
Day 27 grab a cord, grab a cord next to you   109
Day 28 giving back   111
Day 29 what's your pattern   113
Day 30 foundation recap   115
Day 31 launching   119

APPENDIX   123

This workbook is dedicated to our brave youth and adults who have taken a seat in our offices and told their stories of pain, addiction, suffering, abuse, hurt, abandonment, and loneliness. We admire the tears you shared, the stories you told, and the chains that you continue to choose to break in your lives. We thank you for allowing us, as therapists, to be a part of your journey in life that we will never forget.

To our family, friends, and those who have supported us in our journey, we thank you for your sacrifice, love, and time that you have given us. Together you have blessed us with your kindness, wisdom, guidance, and dedication to our ministry.

We thank God, our Heavenly Father, who has blessed us with the vision, passion, and creativity to minister to his children. Your grace and mercy in our own journey have taught us how to care for own emotional and mental health. Thank you.

Do not conform to the pattern of this world, but be transformed by the renewing of your mind. Then you will be able to test and approve what God's will is—his good, pleasing and perfect will.
Romans 12:2-12 (NIV)

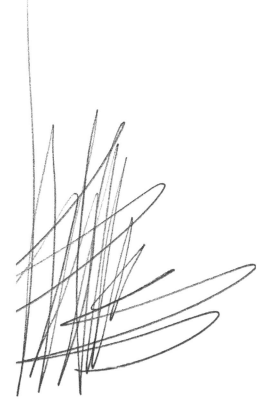

welcome.

Welcome to the best version of YOU!

We are so excited you're here. The toughest part with any sort of change is making the choice to start and following through with it. And since you are reading this text right now, you have started. Congrats! You have begun the process of transforming your mind and heart. Just by opening up this workbook and reading it, you already have a small win to celebrate. You are on your way to becoming the master of your emotions. You are off to a good start!

Yes, there will be challenges, there will be frustrations, and at times you may feel like it's just too hard. You may even feel you're alone, but you're not alone in your anxiety and depression. We have all struggled with symptoms of anxiety and depression. Yes, even us the professionals, the authors of this book. We made available in the appendix a thorough look at what depression and anxiety is.

This workbook is a tool to help care for the symptoms of anxiety and depression that will take you from a place of crisis to clarity. You may struggle to stay focused and to follow-through, but don't worry, it's normal when making the decision to change your life. Stick with it. Stick with the process. You can't grow without some adversity and struggles. It's a good sign your mind and heart are fighting for the best version of you.

"Do not conform to the pattern of this world, but be **transformed** by **the renewing of your mind.** Then you will be able to test and approve what God's will is – his good, pleasing and perfect will." Romans 12:2 (NIV)

Read it again. Now one more time. Yes, three times. This will be your theme verse during this process of emotional transformation. When you feel you want to give up, go back to this and read it. Get a sticky note or a notecard and write Romans 12:2 down and place it on your mirror or maybe on the dashboard of your car. You need to remember this: True emotional transformation cannot occur outside of God. The renewing of the mind comes from the truths and promises of God's word.

This journey of Emotional Transformation will guide you through establishing three critical foundations in your life to help you: Reset, Renew and Restore. These three foundations will provide the support you need to experience ongoing and sustainable change.

Reset You will learn practical ways to reset your emotions by understanding how your emotions can be useful and manageable instead of incontrollable and harmful.

Renew You will learn to renew your mind by paying attention to your thoughts, learning to stop negative self-talk and replace it with Truth.

Restore You will learn to restore your spirit by turning chaos in your life into order through prioritizing your relationship with God.

Go ahead and spend some time in prayer. Ask God for healing. Ask Him for the strength to get through this process. Ask Him for understanding and knowledge, as you are about to embark on this daily journey of Emotional Transformation.

*Side note: In the back of the book we have an Appendix. In the appendix you will find a variety of tools and resources that will be in addition to what we are discussing in the workbook. We suggest you visit them before you start the process.

It is important to find a time during the day to spend on the worksheets and to do The Reset Basics. Commit to a time, whether that's before you leave for school or work, your lunch break, or before bed. Most importantly, we want you to fit this into whatever time best works for your life and schedule, but our preference is that you start your day off with a renewed mindset. *Routine is so important in transforming your mind.*

TIME: _____   **PLACE:** _____

your cord.

As specialists in emotional transformation, we believe that continual change cannot occur without the support, love, and prayers of trustworthy people in your life. The Bible paints an accurate picture of this:

"A person standing alone can be attacked and defeated, but two can stand back-to-back and conquer. Three are even better, for a triple-braided cord is not easily broken."
Ecclesiastes 4:12 (NLT)

This verse beautifully describes the importance of community. We are not meant to go through life alone. We need others in our life to support and help strengthen us in times of trial and defeat.

Think of three people in your life that you would like to come alongside to support you during this time of transformation. We will call these people your Cord. Your Cord needs to be three spiritually mature people in your life that you can trust. It can be family, friends, a mentor, etc. Your Cord will need to commit to you through daily prayer, accountability, and frequent check-ins. These people are going to be welcomed into your journey.

MY CORD:

1. _____

2. _____

3. _____

Go contact your Cord right now. Make the texts or calls you need to get your Cord on board with you!

the daily reset

The Daily Reset are things you need to do every day no matter how you are feeling. This will create consistency. The Daily Reset will help you not only survive, but thrive. You need to have momentum to win the day and to help manage your emotions. Just like when riding a bike, if you stop pedaling you fall over. If you don't continue with The Daily Reset, you will lose your drive in your day. Although, some of these may seem elementary, if you do these things consistently, you will begin to build a solid foundation. This solid foundation will help you no matter what life throws at you.

Here are the things that should be completed in the RESET journal:

name it: journaling.

Every day you will write a letter to God. Tell God how you are feeling and what is going on in your life at that moment. It is an opportunity for you to detox your emotions and lay it at his feet. Be honest with how you are truly feeling. If you are feeling good, be thankful and rejoice in that. If you are feeling anxious or downcast, write it out.

Why is this important? If you don't write it out, you will act it out. Examples of acting it out- (defensive mechanisms) can be found in the appendix. When writing to God, it gives you the control over your emotions versus your emotions controlling you. It allows you to tame your feelings. This will give you perspective on your situation. And God then has an opportunity to intervene. When you write, it becomes a shared experience with God. It practices vulnerability and initiates emotional intelligence (EQ).

rate it: rating your emotions.

Every day, we want you to wake up and rate your overall mood 1-10. 1 being poor and 10 being great. Why is this important? It is important to rate how we are feeling everyday because it will help you to:

1. check-in.
2. measure long-term improvement.
3. claim it.
4. recognize the patterns of your moods.

14

3-2-1 Q's: three questions every morning.

THREE THINGS I'M THANKFUL FOR

1.

2.

3.

TWO THINGS I'M EXCITED ABOUT

1.

2.

ONE THING I WANT TO ACCOMPLISH TODAY

1.

Our hope is that the routine of answering these questions will immediately shift the paradigm of your day. No matter what mood you wake up in, you start your day going from a place of abundance and thankfulness of what you already have in your life, as opposed to what you don't have. Gratefulness is one of the many antidotes to anxiety and depression. It shifts your mind to being strength based versus critic based. Being positive versus being negative.

make a connection: build community.

Every day you must choose to connect with someone: a friend, a family member, a co-worker, or significant other. We encourage connection to not be through your pain or your chaos, but through empathy (understanding others), affirming (building up others), celebrating (encouraging others), or appreciating (recognizing others). This can be seen through having coffee with a friend, to sending a thank you text to a family member, to celebrating a co-worker's success, to giving a compliment.

Why is this important? This is important because anxiety and depression naturally makes you reclusive. God made us to be in dialogue with others, not in a monologue by ourselves. God made us to be expressive and relational, not independent, but to be interdependent.

every week

exercise: just do it.

It has been proven over and over again that getting outside and exercising more days than not, elevates mood, gives healthy perspective, gives you a feeling of accomplishment, and it is a great a coping skill for anxiety and depression. It is not about the intensity or level of exercise. A simple 20-minute walk is a great example. A body in motion makes brain transformation.

foundation recap: check-in with yourself.

At the end of every foundation we would like for you to spend some time reflecting where your emotional equity was spent. It's imperative to recognize any patterns that you would like to change in order to bring more balance to your emotional life. We have also included a Heart Inventory Questionnaire. This gives you another opportunity to assess your progress.

Take a moment and fill out the Heart Inventory Questionnaire on the opposite page!

heart inventory.

The Heart Inventory is comprised of 15 questions that will help you better understand how you're doing through this emotional transformation journey. Answer the following questions as you feel today. On a scale from 1-4 with 1 being "Never" and 4 representing "Always", fill in the circle of the number that represents how you currently feel.

	1	2	3	4
Do you feel hopeful?	①	②	③	④
Do you feel connected to others?	①	②	③	④
Do you feel you are progressing?	①	②	③	④
Do you feel happy?	①	②	③	④
Do you feel in control of your feelings?	①	②	③	④
Do you feel closer to God?	①	②	③	④
Is your positive self-talk increasing?	①	②	③	④
Are you getting enough sleep?	①	②	③	④
Are you exercising regularly?	①	②	③	④
Are you practicing thankfulness?	①	②	③	④
Are you focusing your mind on the present?	①	②	③	④
Do you feel at peace with self?	①	②	③	④
Are you finding ways to serve others?	①	②	③	④
Are you choosing a positive attitude?	①	②	③	④
Do you have control of your thoughts?	①	②	③	④

Total of all the filled in numbers: _____

Now turn the page!

If the total to your Heart Inventory is from:

15-29:
This indicates you may be struggling more than feeling encouraged. This is normal and all part of the process! When feeling overwhelmed review The Daily Resets and spend time revisiting the worksheets in this foundation.

30-36:
This indicates that you may be struggling but change is occurring and your hope is increasing! Keep the momentum going and praise God!

37+:
This indicates hope and change are occurring! You are doing it! Keep doing what you are doing because it is working!

reset emotions.

daily reset

MY OVERALL MOOD: circle one

(poor)   (great)

1   2   3   4   5   6   7   8   9   10

THREE THINGS I'M
THANKFUL FOR

1.

2.

3.

TWO THINGS I'M
EXCITED ABOUT

1.

2.

ONE THING I WANT
TO ACCOMPLISH TODAY

1.

DEAR GOD ...

_____

_____

_____

_____

_____

_____

_____

MY CONNECTION TODAY ⟶

day one.

name it and claim it

"Like an open city with no defenses is the man with no check on his feelings."
Proverbs 25:28 (NAB)

As therapists, the Scripture above is one of our favorites. We love the message of this verse: We all have feelings, our feelings are important for us to understand, and if we don't check or manage our feelings then our feelings will control us. The three common ways that people respond to their emotions: they blame, they complain or they claim. The best choice is obvious: claim it. When we claim how we feel, we are able to take ownership of it. We want to hold the power to control our feelings versus our feelings controlling us.

Do you know God has feelings? We see in Scripture God has compassion, love, anger, grief, and jealousy (Genesis 6:6, Exodus 34:5-6, 32:10, 1 John 4:8). Yes, even jealousy! He is jealous for us (Exodus 34:14). He wants us, all of us! Our God is an emotional God. It makes sense why he equips us with so many emotions. He has feelings just like us.

So, it is critical to know our feelings are not wrong; but how we respond or react to our feelings can be wrong. Unchecked feelings can eventually cause us to be paralyzed. Which may play out in losing a job, unhealthy relationships, or having the inability to attend school, church or other healthy activities. We need to find a way to manage and check our emotions on a regular basis. The more we can identify our feelings, understand them, and put them in check, the healthier we will be.

TURN THE PAGE FOR
TODAY'S ACTIVITY!

Below is a list of unwanted feelings, that if left ignored could be misunderstood and harmful. Take your time, read through the list. Then circle the unwanted emotions you feel you need help managing currently.

Tip: Don't over think it. Choose as many emotions as you currently feel.

Aggressive	Angry	Annoyed	Anxious	Arrogant	Ashamed
Bashful	Bitter	Bored	Broken	Bullied	Cautious
Chaotic	Compulsive	Conceited	Confused	Controlled	Cowardly
Defeated	Dependent	Depressed	Despair	Desperate	Destructive
Detached	Disappointed	Discourage	Disgusted	Doubt	Embarrassed
Enraged	Envious	Exasperated	Exhausted	Fearful	Frightened
Frustrated	Greedy	Grieved	Guilty	Helpless	Hopeless
Hurt	Impatient	Impulsive	Irresponsible	Irritable	Isolated
Jealous	Judged	Lazy	Lonely	Lost	Mad
Manipulated	Miserable	Moody	Negative	Obsessed	Overwhelmed
Pained	Panicked	Paranoid	Perfectionist	Possessive	Powerless
Pride	Puzzled	Regretful	Resentful	Sad	Secretive
Shame	Shocked	Shy	Sorry	Stress	Stupid
Stubborn	Tension	Vengeance	Victimized	Withdrawn	Worry

List below the emotions you circled:

0   10

_____ |—+—+—+—+—|—+—+—+—+—|

_____ |—+—+—+—+—|—+—+—+—+—|

_____ |—+—+—+—+—|—+—+—+—+—|

_____ |—+—+—+—+—|—+—+—+—+—|

_____ |—+—+—+—+—|—+—+—+—+—|

_____ |—+—+—+—+—|—+—+—+—+—|

_____ |—+—+—+—+—|—+—+—+—+—|

_____ |—+—+—+—+—|—+—+—+—+—|

_____ |—+—+—+—+—|—+—+—+—+—|

_____ |—+—+—+—+—|—+—+—+—+—|

_____ |—+—+—+—+—|—+—+—+—+—|

_____ |—+—+—+—+—|—+—+—+—+—|

_____ |—+—+—+—+—|—+—+—+—+—|

_____ |—+—+—+—+—|—+—+—+—+—|

Next to each emotion rate (1-10) the intensity of the emotion with (1) being the least and (10) being the most intense. The importance of tracking the intensity of the emotion helps give you an understanding if the emotion is becoming less or more manageable as you go through this workbook.

Side note: As you go through the workbook some of these emotions may increase intensity as you work through some of the worksheets. If this happens this is normal. Just like a cold, it may get worse before it gets better. Our brain is stubborn and does not want to quickly change. So, stick with it. Don't give up. And just know you are not alone on this. We all have unwanted emotions.

daily reset

MY OVERALL MOOD: circle one

(poor)

(great)

1   2   3   4   5   6   7   8   9   10

THREE THINGS I'M
THANKFUL FOR

1.

2.

3.

TWO THINGS I'M
EXCITED ABOUT

1.

2.

ONE THING I WANT
TO ACCOMPLISH TODAY

1.

DEAR GOD ...

MY CONNECTION TODAY ⟶

day two.

where do you feel it?

At times you can feel your anxiety or depression physically. Based on the feelings you circled in the "Name It and Claim It" exercise, your body may be responding to these feelings physically. At times your body tells you what you are feeling before you mentally recognize your feelings. God gave us these physical cues to help us in identifying our emotions. The more physically and mentally connected we are with our feelings the more empowered we can be, the more strength we have to change it, and the more we can have compassion and grace for it. We are then able to depict whether there is truth to the emotion, as well as, acknowledging the impact of its influence.

On the next page, you'll color in any parts of the body you feel your emotions physically using red or blue colored pencils (or markers) to identify any sensations or pains.

explain where & how
you physically feel your emotions:

Color in any parts of the body you feel your emotions physically using red (warm/hot) or blue (cool/cold) colored pencils to identify any sensations or pains.

After writing and coloring your physical responses to your emotions, what did you learn about how your body responds to your negative emotions?

daily reset

MY OVERALL MOOD: circle one

(poor)   (great)

1   2   3   4   5   6   7   8   9   10

THREE THINGS I'M
THANKFUL FOR

1.

2.

3.

TWO THINGS I'M
EXCITED ABOUT

1.

2.

ONE THING I WANT
TO ACCOMPLISH TODAY

1.

DEAR GOD ...

_____

_____

_____

_____

_____

_____

_____

MY CONNECTION TODAY ⟶

day three.

what worries you?

Whether life is going great or you feel like you're crawling through it, worry seems to creep up like an unwanted companion. On our best days, worry can remind us of how "this will all fall apart…don't get too attached", and on our worst days, worry taunts us to believe that "this will never change."

Worry and anxiety are interchangeable words that simply mean we're kinda freakin' out because we just don't know what might happen, or not happen. We have a tendency to want to be in control, and if we're not in-control we're doing our best to get control.

The Bible talks a lot about worry, perhaps one of the most well-known verses is Philippians 4:6-7:

Do not be anxious about anything, but in every situation,
by prayer and petition, with thanksgiving, present your requests to God.
And the peace of God, which transcends all understanding,
will guard your hearts and your minds in Christ Jesus.
Philippians 4:6-7 (NIV)

You might be saying, "Seriously, don't be anxious about anything !?!" "How!?!"

Let's turn the page and find out using a 3-step process, Claim, Cope and Connect

Step 1: Claim.

Acknowledge your worries. List them out (we've provided note pages in the back of the book where you can write your list)

Step 2: Cope.

Choose to direct your worries towards God. Worry and anxiety grow in power and strength the more we feed them. Instead, we can acknowledge (don't avoid your worries) and bring them before God through prayer- talk to God about what's on your mind and heart

Step 3: Connect.

God wants us to trust Him. We might not have all the answers but by acknowledging that you are giving Him control, you are allowing yourself to connect to His peace. This peace is then promised to Guard our Hearts and Minds so that we don't continue to spiral back into grasping for control.

Remember that God isn't a genie, He wants to connect with us. Prayer is committed time, whether in the car, taking a shower, on a run or brushing our teeth that we are shifting from not just talking to ourselves or a friend, but taking our worries to the one who we trust to be in-control.

"repeat steps 1-3 forever."

(cue *The Sandlot*)

Check back into your list periodically to document how God has answered your prayers.

daily reset

MY OVERALL MOOD: circle one

(poor)   (great)

1   **2**   **3**   **4**   **5**   **6**   **7**   **8**   **9**   **10**

THREE THINGS I'M
THANKFUL FOR

1.

2.

3.

TWO THINGS I'M
EXCITED ABOUT

1.

2.

ONE THING I WANT
TO ACCOMPLISH TODAY

1.

DEAR GOD ...

_____

_____

_____

_____

_____

_____

_____

MY CONNECTION TODAY ⟶

day four.

let's get artsy

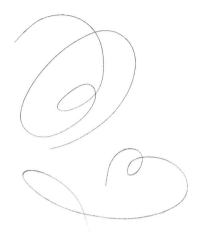

In the "Name It and Claim it" exercise, you circled many emotions you are currently feeling. Write each emotion that you circled on top of a blank page in the back of the workbook. Then on those pages draw out those emotions. It is not about being an artist. Don't focus on making it look perfect or pretty, focus on the intensity of how you are feeling as you draw out your emotions.

Giving your brain the freedom to express your unwanted emotions through creativity is a great exercise to detox unwanted emotions because it activates the right side of the brain. When the right side of the brain is activated, your brain shifts from being logical to being expressive, which allows you to break the cycle of toxic thinking.

The more often you write it out, talk it out, or draw it out, the more often you will be in control of your emotions. Complacency creates dysfunction. You have to work it out. Unresolved emotions will morph into deeper, darker emotions. And preservation of unwanted emotions is exactly what the enemy wants, because the weight of holding onto those emotions causes us defeat and despair.

Feel free to do this on a daily basis or as needed. The less you hold onto emotionally and the more you express it, the healthier you will feel.

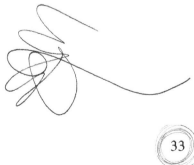

daily reset

MY OVERALL MOOD: circle one

(poor)   (great)

1   2   3   4   5   6   7   8   9   10

THREE THINGS I'M
THANKFUL FOR

1.

2.

3.

TWO THINGS I'M
EXCITED ABOUT

1.

2.

ONE THING I WANT
TO ACCOMPLISH TODAY

1.

DEAR GOD ...

_____

_____

_____

_____

_____

_____

_____

MY CONNECTION TODAY ———⟶

day five.

grounded!

Don't worry, you didn't just hear your mom yelling at you. Being grounded doesn't always have to be a bad thing. Truth is, we all walk around like little automatic machines-thinking, feeling, doing … thinking, feeling doing … Our thoughts and feelings can become so instinctual that we're not even paying attention to the fact that we've been physically present but mentally a hundred miles away.

Well, we're gonna wake you up a bit by walking through some grounding techniques to help your mind come back to reality; what's happening here and now. Sometimes we "checkout" because we feel overwhelmed. This technique reminds us that being present can actually help us in at least two specific ways 1. We can recognize what about our immediate situation is good, safe and comfortable and 2. We can better access our strengths, skills and knowledge.

We have 5 senses: Sight, Smell, Touch, Taste and Hearing. Those 5 senses serve to better connect us to our environment. When we feel overwhelmed, anxious, depressed, etc. we can connect to our senses to reconnect our mind with our body.

To practice grounding yourself at any time, consider these 5 senses…

Sight
Silently, or out loud (but don't be a weirdo) list off things you can see around you.

Sound
What do you hear? Try and quiet your mind to hear even the faintest noise.

Touch
What do you feel? Are you sitting or standing? If possible, take your shoes off and feel the grass or carpet beneath you. You could also find an object around you like a smooth rock, or some ice.

Taste
Do you taste anything? Even if you're not eating or drinking, sometimes you can just have a bad taste in your mouth.

Smell
What do you smell around you? Warning: this could get sketchy.

daily reset

MY OVERALL MOOD: circle one

(poor)   (great)

1   2   3   4   5   6   7   8   9   10

THREE THINGS I'M
THANKFUL FOR

1.

2.

3.

TWO THINGS I'M
EXCITED ABOUT

1.

2.

ONE THING I WANT
TO ACCOMPLISH TODAY

1.

DEAR GOD ...

_____

_____

_____

_____

_____

_____

_____

MY CONNECTION TODAY ⟶

day six.

perspective shift

Sometimes we can walk outside and the sky seems like a crisp blue, the birds are chirping and the sun seems to be particularly cozy and then there's those other days where that same blue sky seems annoyingly bright, the birds are squawking more than chirping and the sun is beating down on us.

It's ALL about perspective. How we see ourselves, our friendships/relationships around us and our future, determine our days.

1st. Write down three ways you view yourself.

1) _____

2) _____

3) _____

Next. Write 3 ways those views affect your relationships.

1) _____

2) _____

3) _____

Finally. Write 3 ways you want to view yourself in the future.

1) _____

2) _____

3) _____

Were those traits critical or compassionate? Encouraging or discouraging?

When we see ourselves with compassion, we see others with that same perspective. Our future, as a result, seems more like the crisp blue sky than annoyingly bright.

Check out Joy healers and Joy stealers in the appendix to further help shift your perspective (pg. 136).

daily reset

MY OVERALL MOOD: circle one

(poor)

1   2   3   4   5   6   7   8   9   10   (great)

THREE THINGS I'M
THANKFUL FOR

1.

2.

3.

TWO THINGS I'M
EXCITED ABOUT

1.

2.

ONE THING I WANT
TO ACCOMPLISH TODAY

1.

DEAR GOD ...

_____

_____

_____

_____

_____

_____

_____

MY CONNECTION TODAY ⎯⎯⎯→

day seven.

fun : *[noun]* enjoyment, amusement or lighthearted pleasure

What do you like to do for fun? We challenge you to do something, anything that you find fun!

Here are some random ideas to get you thinking. Feel free to steal any, we won't know!

- Play a board game
- Go for a bike ride
- Get ice cream
- Take a day off
- Binge watch your favorite show
- Spend an extra day perfecting your hobby (fishing, skiing, playing the piano, you get the idea)
- Become an amateur photographer for a day
- Gather some wild flowers to make your own bouquet
- Have coffee or dessert or both, with a friend
- Go for a hike
- Take a drive with no destination in mind and blair some FUN music
- Watch a movie
- Try a new restaurant out
- Have a Lego building contest
- Host an impromptu BBQ
- Stay up late or tuck-in early
- Watch the sunset
- Sit outside by a fire, for extra credit, make s'mores
- Share most embarrassing stories with family and friends
- Get pampered

Now it's your turn, think of 3 of your own ideas:

_____   _____   _____

*keep it legal, respectable and ethical. Something that Jesus would give a thumbs-up to.

daily reset

MY OVERALL MOOD: circle one

(poor)   (great)

1   2   3   4   5   6   7   8   9   10

THREE THINGS I'M
THANKFUL FOR

1.

2.

3.

TWO THINGS I'M
EXCITED ABOUT

1.

2.

ONE THING I WANT
TO ACCOMPLISH TODAY

1.

DEAR GOD ...

_____

_____

_____

_____

_____

_____

_____

MY CONNECTION TODAY ——→

day eight.

foundation recap

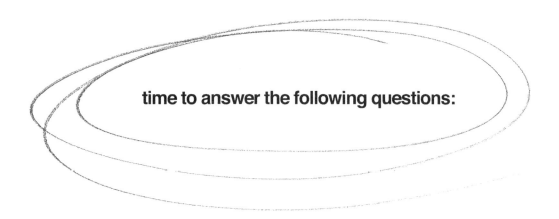

time to answer the following questions:

Where did you spend your emotional energy?

Did you learn anything new about yourself?

What new techniques helped you?

What did your journaling reveal to you?

Have you checked in with your Cord recently? Yes or No (If no, text or call them right now!)

---

heart inventory

The Heart Inventory is comprised of 15 questions that will help you better understand how you're doing through this emotional transformation journey. Answer the following questions as you feel today. On a scale from 1-4 with 1 being "Never" and 4 representing "Always", circle the number that represents how you currently feel.

fill in a number: 1= never 4= always

	1	2	3	4
Do you feel hopeful?	①	②	③	④
Do you feel connected to others?	①	②	③	④
Do you feel you are progressing?	①	②	③	④
Do you feel happy?	①	②	③	④
Do you feel in control of your feelings?	①	②	③	④
Do you feel closer to God?	①	②	③	④
Is your positive self-talk increasing?	①	②	③	④
Are you getting enough sleep?	①	②	③	④
Are you exercising regularly?	①	②	③	④
Are you practicing thankfulness?	①	②	③	④
Are you focusing your mind on the present?	①	②	③	④
Do you feel more at peace with self?	①	②	③	④
Are you finding ways to serve others?	①	②	③	④
Are you choosing a positive attitude?	①	②	③	④
Do you have control of your thoughts?	①	②	③	④

Total of all the filled in numbers: _____

If the total to your Heart Inventory is from:

15-29:
This indicates you may be struggling more than feeling encouraged. This is normal and all part of the process! When feeling overwhelmed review The Daily Resets and spend time revisiting the worksheets in this foundation.

30-36:
This indicates that you may be struggling but change is occurring and your hope is increasing! Keep the momentum going and praise God!

37+:
This indicates hope and change are occurring! You are doing it! Keep doing what you are doing because it is working!

renew mind.

daily reset

MY OVERALL MOOD: circle one

(poor)   (great)

1   2   3   4   5   6   7   8   9   10

THREE THINGS I'M
THANKFUL FOR

1.

2.

3.

TWO THINGS I'M
EXCITED ABOUT

1.

2.

ONE THING I WANT
TO ACCOMPLISH TODAY

1.

DEAR GOD ...

_____

_____

_____

_____

_____

_____

_____

MY CONNECTION TODAY ⟶

day nine.

self-talk

You may or may not know this but everyone has an internal dialogue that is happening all the time. Since you are going through this book, you are quite aware of it. Sometimes it becomes defeating, self-deprecating and negative. For a lot of us it's one of the big hurdles to getting us to a healthier relationship with ourselves. Self-talk is where negative thoughts and behaviors are triggered. It is where panic and anxiety attacks, eating disorders, self-destructive thoughts, unrealistic fears, cutting, suicidal thoughts and the beginnings of sabotaging healthy relationships are born.

So, what we'd like to do is teach you how to reconstruct your self-talk through a variety of exercises and worksheets designed to change your style of thinking. To start let's make a list of all the ways your self-talk can lie to you. List out the negative thoughts your "inner-bully" tells you that feel real but are wrong or mean. These might be things like "I am never good enough." "No one likes me." "People don't notice me."

Take some time now and write out your negative self-talk and the lies your inner bully tells you everyday:

_____

_____

_____

_____

_____

_____

_____

_____

daily reset

MY OVERALL MOOD: circle one

(poor)   (great)

1   2   3   4   5   6   7   8   9   10

THREE THINGS I'M
THANKFUL FOR

1.

2.

3.

TWO THINGS I'M
EXCITED ABOUT

1.

2.

ONE THING I WANT
TO ACCOMPLISH TODAY

1.

DEAR GOD ...

_____

_____

_____

_____

_____

_____

_____

MY CONNECTION TODAY ———⟶

day ten.

stinking thinking

There is nothing worse than racing negative thoughts that you can't control. They keep you up all night or just ruin your day.

We call that stinking thinking. To help manage such thoughts we came up with an exercise to help control them. Write down on the left side of the chart all of the stinking thinking (negative self-talk) surrounding your anxiety or depression. Then on the right side where it says "Alternative Thinking", write down the opposite or positive thought for each Stinking Thinking thought. These are statements that begin with **"I am,"** and **"I will"** –no **"can't,"** **"won't,"** or **"don't"** statements. Feel free to have more than one Alternative Thought per Stinking Thinking Thought. After you are done, say out loud the Alternative Thoughts ten times through. Circle the one thought that gave you the most peace or motivation. Then write that thought below the chart where it says "Mantra".

Now every time you have a stinking thinking thought, tell yourself "STOP" and replace the negative thought with the mantra and say it over and over again until you feel relief. This is a great way to quiet our inner bully that we all have.

Tip: Use the example on the next page to help you on the format of this exercise!

stinking thinking (negative thoughts)	alternative thinking (positive thoughts)
I'M NOT GOOD LOOKING	I AM BEAUTIFULLY MADE BY GOD
No ONE LIKES ME	I WILL TELL MYSELF I AM BEAUTIFUL EVERYDAY
I'M BETTER OFF DEAD	I WILL HAVE GREAT FRIENDSHIPS
I'M NOT A GOOD PERSON	I WILL BE A GOOD FRIEND TO OTHERS
I'M GOING TO FAIL	I WILL TREAT OTHERS WELL
I'M STUPID	I DO HAVE A PURPOSE IN LIFE
	I WILL BE USED BY GOD
	I AM MORE VALUABLE ALIVE
	I WILL CELEBRATE OTHER PEOPLE
	I WILL AFFIRM OTHERS
	I WILL USE MY WORDS TO BLESS OTHERS
	I WILL BE SUCCESSFUL IN WHAT I DO
	I WILL PRACTICE AND PREPARE FOR MY TASK
	I WILL USE FAILURES AS OPPORTUNITIES TO LEARN
	I WILL PRAISE GOD REGARDLESS OF THE RESULT
	I AM SMART ENOUGH
	I AM CAPABLE

mantra   I DO HAVE A PURPOSE IN LIFE

stinking thinking
(negative thoughts)

alternative thinking
(positive thoughts)

mantra _____

daily reset

MY OVERALL MOOD: circle one

(poor)   (great)

1   2   3   4   5   6   7   8   9   10

THREE THINGS I'M
THANKFUL FOR

1.

2.

3.

TWO THINGS I'M
EXCITED ABOUT

1.

2.

ONE THING I WANT
TO ACCOMPLISH TODAY

1.

DEAR GOD ...

_____

_____

_____

_____

_____

_____

_____

MY CONNECTION TODAY ⟶

day eleven.

how your thoughts lie to you

Now let's go a little deeper on our Stinking Thinking. One thing you need to understand is your depression or anxiety lies to you. It tells you things about yourself or others that are not true. It is important for you to recognize those lies and not believe the toxic thoughts that can come from them. Some of the lies we often hear from people we work with are:

- *I'm not good enough*
- *I'm never going to get better*
- *No one loves me or will ever love me*
- *I will never be good enough*
- *I will never find a job or get into school*
- *I am better off alone*
- *I feel I am failing life*
- *I am a horrible spouse, parent, or friend.*
- *God can't use me*

The hard part is these lies can feel real and can take something that is a kernel of truth and make it into your identity and give you great insecurities. So, let's take some time and make a list of the lies your anxiety and/or depression says to you:

Looking back at the Stinking Thinking worksheet and the list of lies from today, and use the blank page to write out and process:

What themes or patterns are being revealed?

When was the first time you felt or heard these lies? How old were you?

What or who reinforces these lies to make you believe them?

There are two ways we feel you can break the cycle of believing in these lies:

Tell God: Give God your thoughts and feelings in prayer. Let him know about your stinking thinking and the lies that come from them. Ask the Holy Spirit (the great counselor) to give you wisdom and discernment on what is truth.

Tell your Cord: You are as sick as your secrets are. Secrets are what preserve lies. Secrets are what preserve stinking thinking. Call your Cord and let them know the stinkin' thinkin' you struggle with, and the consequences that come from your pattern of stinking thinking. Then ask them to pray over you. Confession to God and expression to others are ultimate disruptors to this cycle.

daily reset

MY OVERALL MOOD: circle one

(poor)   (great)

1   2   3   4   5   6   7   8   9   10

THREE THINGS I'M
THANKFUL FOR

1.

2.

3.

TWO THINGS I'M
EXCITED ABOUT

1.

2.

ONE THING I WANT
TO ACCOMPLISH TODAY

1.

DEAR GOD ...

_____

_____

_____

_____

_____

_____

_____

_____

MY CONNECTION TODAY ———→

day twelve.

the "what if" technique

More often than not your thoughts talk you out of the good and into the bad. It comes from a style of thinking that we call "What If":

- *What if I fail?*
- *What if I don't get the job?*
- *What if I don't get married?*
- *What if I don't get into college?*
- *What if I'm a horrible parent?*

"What If" are two words that can either be the driving force of you being paralyzed emotionally or being motivated. The difference between the two is quite simple. Instead of using "What If" in terms of worse case scenarios, you instead use "What If" in the best-case scenarios. The exercise below is a great tool that you can use when you have feelings of doubt, insecurity or performance anxiety. Look over the example and then fill-in your own "What If" statements in the worksheet provided.

Paralyzing What-If	Motivating What-If
WHAT IF I FAIL AT GETTING A JOB	WHAT IF I AM SUCCESSFUL AT GETTING A JOB
	WHAT IF I PREPARE MYSELF FOR THE INTERVIEW
	WHAT IF I LEAVE THE INTERVIEW FEELING CONFIDENT
	WHAT IF I GO IN THERE SMILING AND GIVING GOOD EYE CONTACT
	WHAT IF I GET PAID MORE THAN WHAT I AM WANTING

Paralyzing What-If   ## Motivating What-If

day twelve is over, but here's a page that is 100% yours to do with it whatever you want. maybe see if you can remember all fifty states, cover it in glitter glue, maybe draw a unicorn or ninjas fighting pirates, or maybe leave it blank. seriously ... your call ... but we vote ninjas ...

daily reset

MY OVERALL MOOD: circle one

(poor)   (great)

1   2   3   4   5   6   7   8   9   10

THREE THINGS I'M
THANKFUL FOR

1.

2.

3.

TWO THINGS I'M
EXCITED ABOUT

1.

2.

ONE THING I WANT
TO ACCOMPLISH TODAY

1.

DEAR GOD ...

_____

_____

_____

_____

_____

_____

_____

MY CONNECTION TODAY ——→

day thirteen.

attitude of gratitude

The Bible tells us that we have the ability to control our thoughts and as a result, "renew" our mind. We believe that thoughts lead to feelings and feelings lead to behavior. Therefore, it would be extremely imperative to spend time shaping how we think. Just as a little cancer can permeate and destroy our body, the diseases of anger, bitterness, fear, and sadness can wreak havoc on our souls. Luckily, there are treatments that can send these thought cancers into remission. One of these soul-restoring treatments is (as you probably gathered from the title) having an attitude of gratitude. This is not a controversial, new development. In fact, this is something that Christian and non-Christian communities actually agree: dwelling on what we are grateful for can actually change (for the positive) our outlook of the world, our mood, and even our physical health. But, by all means, don't take my word for it:

> *"See that no one repays anyone evil for evil, but always seek to do good to one another and to everyone. Rejoice always, pray without ceasing, give thanks in all circumstances; for this is the will of God in Christ Jesus for you."*
> 1 Thess. 5:15-18

You may be asking yourself, "Well, I want an attitude of gratitude. How do I get one?" Here are some steps that will get you on your way:

1. Through prayer, ask God to open your eyes to even the small things that we can be grateful for. (i.e. I have food to eat, I got out of bed today, I can hear the birds chirping)

2. Continue to spend 5-10 minutes daily writing down a few things that you noticed throughout the day you are thankful for. This is why we have it as part of The Daily Reset.

3. At least once a week, spend time thinking about a person in your life that you are grateful for or has made an impact in your life. It could be a teacher, friend, coach, co-worker, spouse, or… I think you get the idea. If you are an overachiever, you can send one or all of those people an email or even text about how you feel. (Could you imagine getting one from someone?!? Tears)

daily reset

MY OVERALL MOOD: circle one

(poor)   (great)

1   2   3   4   5   6   7   8   9   10

THREE THINGS I'M
THANKFUL FOR

1.

2.

3.

TWO THINGS I'M
EXCITED ABOUT

1.

2.

ONE THING I WANT
TO ACCOMPLISH TODAY

1.

DEAR GOD ...

_____

_____

_____

_____

_____

_____

_____

MY CONNECTION TODAY ⟶

day fourteen.

from monologue to dialogue

The real mastery of self-talk is to go from a monologue with self to a dialogue with God. When all else fails, redirect all negative talk to God. Some people call this prayer walking. It's where a healthy brain is talking, reflecting, brainstorming, connecting and sharing your thoughts with God.

"God, I am having such a hard time right now."
"Lord, I am so anxious every day."
"God, I am scared that I won't get this job."
"Lord, I feel so overwhelmed."

This is a continual dialogue between you and God. One of the beauties of the dialogue is that you can shift from sharing our wounds and stresses to sharing our gratitude and celebrating our relationship with God.

Some ways to connect and dialogue with God can happen through prayer, listening to praise and worship music, getting out in nature or reading scripture.

Why don't you take some time and practice this right now.

daily reset

MY OVERALL MOOD: circle one

(poor)

1   2   3   4   5   6   7   8   9   10

(great)

THREE THINGS I'M
THANKFUL FOR

1.

2.

3.

TWO THINGS I'M
EXCITED ABOUT

1.

2.

ONE THING I WANT
TO ACCOMPLISH TODAY

1.

DEAR GOD ...

_____

_____

_____

_____

_____

_____

_____

MY CONNECTION TODAY ⟶

day fifteen.

small wins

One thing we want to look at is how we're defining improvement. At times we get lost looking at the finish line as the only win, not recognizing that there are so many small wins that lead and add up to The Final Win. For example, if you're struggling with anxiety and don't feel like going to work or school, then you decided to get up, get dressed, show up to work/school and connect with others, you have accomplished four small wins throughout the day despite the original feeling of not wanting to go to work.

A symptom of anxiety and depression is often being hard on yourself. Looking for small wins is an opportunity to look for ways to celebrate you.

A small win is breaking up the goal or task into manageable and achievable moments.

Make a list below of several "small wins" that you can accomplish through your day and week. Make sure to take time to acknowledge your "small wins" by celebrating yourself. It is important to recognize such wins when they come.

Daily Small Wins	Weekly Small Wins
I got up today.	Journaled at least once this week.
I took a shower.	Work out at least once this week.
I went to work or school.	Got to work or school on time.
KEEP ON GOING!	

daily reset

MY OVERALL MOOD: circle one

1   2   3   4   5   6   7   8   9   10

THREE THINGS I'M
THANKFUL FOR

1.

2.

3.

TWO THINGS I'M
EXCITED ABOUT

1.

2.

ONE THING I WANT
TO ACCOMPLISH TODAY

1.

DEAR GOD ...

_____

_____

_____

_____

_____

_____

_____

MY CONNECTION TODAY ⟶

day sixteen.

no more than three

The mind is like an engine, when you run hot, something will break down. Balance is important in a culture where busyness is affirmed and success is measured by how much you've accomplished. It's important that your days don't trigger or overwhelm you emotionally by filling them up with an abundance of tasks. Limiting your daily tasks makes room and equity for your own mental and emotional health. Structure your day in a way that gives you opportunity for interruptions and changes.

Outside of the daily have-to's as a family member, student, or professional that we need to accomplish, we want you to limit yourself to only three things to focus on every day.

To do this you need to write down the boundaries you need to put in place to create a balanced life. When you have boundaries, you are in control of how you feel and what you do. When you don't have boundaries then others are in control of how you feel and what you do.

Write below the boundaries you need in the boxes below!

RELATIONAL	EMOTIONAL
PHYSICAL	OTHER

daily reset

MY OVERALL MOOD: circle one

(poor)

1   2   3   4   5   6   7   8   9   10

(great)

THREE THINGS I'M
THANKFUL FOR

1.

2.

3.

TWO THINGS I'M
EXCITED ABOUT

1.

2.

ONE THING I WANT
TO ACCOMPLISH TODAY

1.

DEAR GOD ...

MY CONNECTION TODAY

day seventeen.

order and chaos

In life things are categorized by order or chaos. Order is defined as things that bring peace, health, connection, growth, stability, and maturity in our lives. Chaos is defined as things that disrupt, disturb, conflict, and create insecurity, brokenness, fear, doubt, hurt, and instability in our lives. When our life is tilted more toward chaos than order, the byproduct results in anxiety and depression.

On the worksheet below list on the left side all the things in your life that create chaos and on the right side list all the things in your life that create order. These may range from, relationships, memories, experiences, behaviors, social media, self-talk, etc.

Creates Chaos	Creates Order

This exercise is to develop a filter that will help you ask the question, "Does this bring chaos or order in my life?" Looking at your worksheet, do you see a common theme with any chaos or order items?

What are ways you can grow your Order list?

```


```

What are ways you can decrease or control items on your Chaos list?

```


```

Action Point: Spend some time in prayer asking God for strength and boundaries on your chaos items.

daily reset

MY OVERALL MOOD: circle one

(poor)

1   2   3   4   5   6   7   8   9   10

(great)

THREE THINGS I'M
THANKFUL FOR

1.

2.

3.

TWO THINGS I'M
EXCITED ABOUT

1.

2.

ONE THING I WANT
TO ACCOMPLISH TODAY

1.

DEAR GOD ...

MY CONNECTION TODAY ⟶

day eighteen.

what are your triggers?

Triggers are something that increases your anxiety or depression. We all have them. It is whether or not you are aware of them. We would like for you to spend some time writing your triggers for your depression or anxiety. Follow the example below and place anxiety or depression in the center. Around the center, write down the ways that this struggle is being triggered. Some of the triggers can be: places, relationships, performances, social media, negative feelings, sound, smell, memories or words, etc. Feel free to do as many webs as needed based on the number of pressing emotional struggles you may be experiencing.

you can use these pages to make as many webs as you would like! don't hold back!

daily reset

MY OVERALL MOOD: circle one

(poor)

1   2   3   4   5   6   7   8   9   10

(great)

THREE THINGS I'M
THANKFUL FOR

1.

2.

3.

TWO THINGS I'M
EXCITED ABOUT

1.

2.

ONE THING I WANT
TO ACCOMPLISH TODAY

1.

DEAR GOD ...

_____

_____

_____

_____

_____

_____

_____

MY CONNECTION TODAY ——→

day nineteen.

trigger antidotes

Below are the Trigger Antidote steps. When you find yourself becoming triggered, this is what we want you to do (remember the 3 C's):

Claim: Recognize it and name it. When you name it you can tame it! You can only manage what you identify in life. And when you name it you can change it. Why? Because you are coming from a place of acceptance.

Action Step. Write out the following questions:

What am I feeling?	What are my triggers? (environment, situation, relationship)

Then write a letter to God.

Cope: What coping skills can you use to help de-escalate your anxiety or depression? Circle below three coping skills find most helpful.

Deep breaths   Positive self-talk   Share your need   Grounding Exercise   Journal

Listen to music   Draw   Squeeze ice   Pray   Read scriptures

Write what you are thankful for   Take a bath or shower   Read a book

Interact with your pet (if applicable)   Eat a healthy snack   Go for a drive (if applicable)

Do a puzzle   Write, draw, paint, photography   Play an instrument, sing, dance, act

Squeeze play-doh   Watch a good movie   Play a board/card game   Laugh

Clean or organize your environment   Read   Lower your expectations of the situation

Keep an inspirational quote with you   Scream in a pillow   Punch a pillow   Cry

Action Step. Do the coping skills until you feel relieved from how you feel.

Connect: Reach out to someone who can offer you support. We urge you to keep sharing, keep revealing. Revealing is healing. If you want change in your life, then reveal how you feel to others. It is broken until it is spoken.

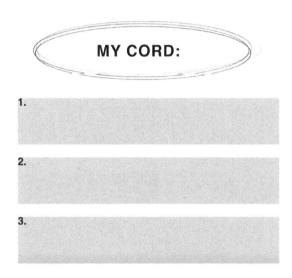

MY CORD:

1.

2.

3.

Action Step. Reach out to your cord and let them know how you are feeling and what is triggering you.

daily reset

MY OVERALL MOOD: circle one

(poor)   (great)

1   2   3   4   5   6   7   8   9   10

THREE THINGS I'M
THANKFUL FOR

1.

2.

3.

TWO THINGS I'M
EXCITED ABOUT

1.

2.

ONE THING I WANT
TO ACCOMPLISH TODAY

1.

DEAR GOD ...

_____

_____

_____

_____

_____

_____

_____

MY CONNECTION TODAY ⟶

day twenty.

where the mind goes the body goes

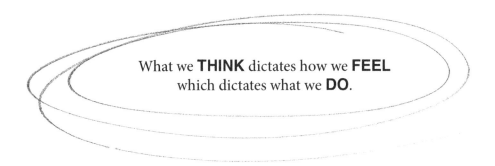

What we **THINK** dictates how we **FEEL** which dictates what we **DO**.

Thinking leads to feeling which leads to doing. Or to put is simply: where the mind goes the body goes. In order to get going and to motivate yourself to do the hard changes that make a difference in emotional transformation, you have to get your mind focused. Sports psychologists tell athletes the difference between a good game and a bad game is your attitude. Meaning, your thinking around the game is critical to the success as an athlete. The same rule applies with being healthy emotionally.

Look back at your Order and Chaos list on Day 17. What comes naturally to us is chaos. Order takes practice. Its takes focus. It takes work. Order begins in the mind….and the body will follow. One of the mistakes people make is they try to resist the chaos or they choose to ignore it. The old saying, "What you resist persists" is true. Instead of resisting, we want you to practice refocusing. Specifically refocusing on God, His love, and His love letter The Bible.

This exercise will feel familiar to the Stinking Thinking worksheet, but this time we will be targeting specific items from your Order list, instead of our thoughts. You have two columns to fill out. Below is an explanation of each column:

Choose an 'Order': Choose one 'Order' from your "Order and Chaos" chart you want to grow more in this week. Just one. It is important to choose one and go deep with it and follow through. For example, it can be working out, meeting a friend, doing your devotions daily, celebrating someone, practicing guitar or just simply getting out of bed the same time every day. You choose.

Supporting Healthy Thoughts: Write down all the supporting and positive thoughts that surround doing and accomplishing the targeted 'Order'. These thoughts should be motivating. We suggest starting these thoughts with "I am" or "I feel" statements. These statements produce healthy self-talk around strengthening the Order you have chosen. Read through the supporting healthy thoughts ten times out loud. Circle the one thought that gives you the most motivation in strengthening the specific Order. Write this down as your mantra.

An 'Order' Item from your list	Healthy thoughts supporting the 'Order'
Exercising Daily	I feel good about myself when I exercise
	I feel more accomplished when I exercise
	I am investing in myself when I exercise
	Exercise helps increase the feel good chemicals in my brain

mantra   I am investing in myself when I exercise

An 'Order' Item from your list	Healthy thoughts supporting the 'Order'

mantra _____

Take it to the cross: Take time each day and ask God in prayer to help you grow and increase the Order in your life. Thank Him for the people, relationships, and behaviors that bring Order to you. Remember without God, Order doesn't exist. Chaos occurs in the absence of God. It is important to prioritize Him in your life. Now you may be asking "How do I do that?". Great question! The next foundation will coach you through it.

daily reset

MY OVERALL MOOD: circle one

(poor)
1 2 3 4 5 6 7 8 9 10
(great)

THREE THINGS I'M
THANKFUL FOR

1.

2.

3.

TWO THINGS I'M
EXCITED ABOUT

1.

2.

ONE THING I WANT
TO ACCOMPLISH TODAY

1.

DEAR GOD ...

MY CONNECTION TODAY ⟶

day twenty one.

foundation recap

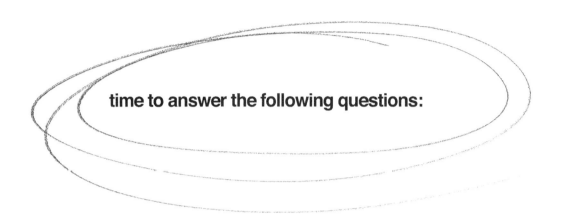

time to answer the following questions:

Where did you spend your emotional energy?

_____

Did you learn anything new about yourself?

_____

What new techniques helped you?

_____

What did your journaling reveal to you?

_____

Have you checked in with your Cord recently? Yes or No (If no, text or call them now!)

_____

heart inventory

The Heart Inventory is comprised of 15 questions that will help you better understand how you're doing through this emotional transformation journey. Answer the following questions as you feel today. On a scale from 1-4 with 1 being "Never" and 4 representing "Always", circle the number that represents how you currently feel.

fill in a number: 1= never 4= always

Do you feel hopeful?	①	②	③	④
Do you feel connected to others?	①	②	③	④
Do you feel you are progressing?	①	②	③	④
Do you feel happy?	①	②	③	④
Do you feel in control of your feelings?	①	②	③	④
Do you feel closer to God?	①	②	③	④
Is your positive self-talk increasing?	①	②	③	④
Are you getting enough sleep?	①	②	③	④
Are you exercising regularly?	①	②	③	④
Are you practicing thankfulness?	①	②	③	④
Are you focusing your mind on the present?	①	②	③	④
Do you feel more at peace with self?	①	②	③	④
Are you finding ways to serve others?	①	②	③	④
Are you choosing a positive attitude?	①	②	③	④
Do you have control of your thoughts?	①	②	③	④

Total of all the filled in numbers: _____

If the total to your Heart Inventory is from:

15-29:
This indicates you may be struggling more than feeling encouraged. This is normal and all part of the process! When feeling overwhelmed review The Daily Resets and spend time revisiting the worksheets in this foundation.

30-36:
This indicates that you may be struggling but change is occurring and your hope is increasing! Keep the momentum going and praise God!

37+:
This indicates hope and change are occurring! You are doing it! Keep doing what you are doing because it is working!

restore spirit.

daily reset

MY OVERALL MOOD: circle one

(poor)

(great)

1   2   3   4   5   6   7   8   9   10

THREE THINGS I'M
THANKFUL FOR

1.

2.

3.

TWO THINGS I'M
EXCITED ABOUT

1.

2.

ONE THING I WANT
TO ACCOMPLISH TODAY

1.

DEAR GOD ...

_____

_____

_____

_____

_____

_____

_____

MY CONNECTION TODAY ⟶

day twenty two.

prioritizing God

We all are yoked or attached to something. If you're not yoked with God, you're yoked with something else. Yoked is a farming term that the Bible uses as a metaphor for two things: how we live our life and how we have good relationships.

A yoke is a wooden device connecting two animals and is used to plow the land. A farmer finds two animals that are of equal strength and size. The animals work as a team to accomplish the goal of plowing the land together in a straight line. But when two animals come together with one animal being weaker or smaller, unequal in strength, what happens is, they go in circles and they don't achieve their goal. Nothing gets done.

So, what's the point? When you're equally yoked with God, you are teamed with God. You are in pace with God and are able to accomplish His goals for you as promised in Matthew 11:28-30:

> "Come to me, all you who are weary and burdened, and I will give you rest. Take my yoke upon you and learn from me, for I am gentle and humble in heart, and you will find rest for your souls. For my yoke is easy and my burden is light."
>
> Matthew 11:28-30 (NIV)

The promise is that, when you take on His easy yoke and light burden by trusting Him, you can rest and He will do the work. God wants us to depend on him and not on ourselves.

The opposite of being yoked with God is being B.U.S.Y. (stands for Being Under Satan's Yoke). Before we come to God, we are weary and burdened. When we become equally yoked with God, our burdens are lifted.

So how can we become yoked with God?

By prioritizing God in making Him first in all areas: in your finances, in your relationships, with your words, with your thoughts, by serving others, instead of choosing to escape you draw near to him by asking God to grow the fruit of the Spirit within you.

Here are common things that get in the way of us prioritizing God:

- Submitting to laziness
- Believing the lies of depression and anxiety
- Surrendering to shame and guilt
- Choosing isolation
- Neglecting church community along with personal growth
- Feeling distant from God

The beauty of prioritizing God is as simple as right now, you saying a prayer, telling God that you want Him to be the number one priority in your life. That step is a small win towards putting God first. Below we started a prayer for you. Finish writing the prayer by letting God know what areas of your life you want him more involved in and what areas of life you need to prioritize him more on.

Dear Lord,
I long to be yoked to you. Help me to put aside anything that is taking your rightful place.

now write or draw your own prayer to God, asking Him to sit on the throne of your heart

daily reset

MY OVERALL MOOD: circle one

(poor)   (great)

1   2   3   4   5   6   7   8   9   10

THREE THINGS I'M
THANKFUL FOR

1.

2.

3.

TWO THINGS I'M
EXCITED ABOUT

1.

2.

ONE THING I WANT
TO ACCOMPLISH TODAY

1.

DEAR GOD ...

_____

_____

_____

_____

_____

_____

_____

MY CONNECTION TODAY ⟶

day twenty three.

drawing near to God

"When my heart was grieved and my spirit embittered, I was senseless and ignorant; I was a brute beast before you. Yet I am always with you; you hold me by my right hand. You guide me with your counsel, and afterward you will take me into glory. Whom have I in heaven but you? And earth has nothing I desire besides you. My flesh and my heart may fail, but God is the strength of my heart and my portion forever. Those who are far from you will perish; you destroy all who are unfaithful to you. But as for me, it is good to be near God. I have made the Sovereign Lord my refuge; I will tell of all your deeds."
Psalms 73:21-28

From this verse we get the following benefits from drawing near to God:
1. He takes you by the hand
2. He guides you with His counsel
3. He walks you into glory
4. He becomes what you focus on instead of what grieves you
5. He becomes the strength of your heart and all you need
6. He gives you confidence
7. He makes you feel "good" to be near Him.

What about the costs from turning away from God? Well, it leads to unmanageable depression, anxiety, bitterness and loneliness.

How can you draw near to God? The answer remains the same as with any relationship, time spent together builds intimacy. Choose to be intentional about talking to God daily. Allow yourself to be vulnerable with Him, as David was, about your current struggles. Seek His guidance. He wants to give it to you. Pray to Him, read His word and plan to attend church weekly. God moves in us when we surround ourselves with His children.

Action Step. This week do what we call "The Two Minute Drill". Before you go to school/work, hang out with friends, start homework, play a sport, etc., take two minutes and give it God in prayer. Ask God to use you and to bless you in what you are about to do. Try this every day, multiple times a day. Be surprised when you start prioritizing God how your emotions and connections with others change.

daily reset

MY OVERALL MOOD: circle one

(poor)   (great)

1   2   3   4   5   6   7   8   9   10

THREE THINGS I'M
THANKFUL FOR

1.

2.

3.

TWO THINGS I'M
EXCITED ABOUT

1.

2.

ONE THING I WANT
TO ACCOMPLISH TODAY

1.

DEAR GOD ...

_____

_____

_____

_____

_____

_____

_____

MY CONNECTION TODAY ⟶

day twenty four.

write a psalm

A psalm is simply a prayer that in Biblical times was used on many occasions as a song. A psalm is an expression of the soul, praising and requesting from God the desires of your heart.

We want you to write your own psalm to share your heart with God. Here is the format of how we want you to write your psalm (write 3-5 sentences for each category):

Praise and Adoration. Praise God and express the attributes that you're thankful for about him (his love, his grace, his mercy, etc.)

Lament and Grieve. Be truthful with your hurts, share your struggles and your pain

Confess and Forgive. Confess areas of sin, stubbornness and doubt, ask for forgiveness for any areas in your life that are in opposition to what God wants for you and ask for strength to change

Praise and gratitude. Praise God and express your gratitude for hearing your heart and for him actively interceding on your behalf

PRAISE/ADORATION

_____

_____

_____

_____

_____

_____

_____

_____

_____

LAMENT/GRIEVE

_____

_____

_____

_____

_____

_____

_____

_____

_____

CONFESS/FORGIVE

PRAISE/GRATITUDE

daily reset

MY OVERALL MOOD: circle one

(poor)

1   2   3   4   5   6   7   8   9   10   (great)

THREE THINGS I'M
THANKFUL FOR

1.

2.

3.

TWO THINGS I'M
EXCITED ABOUT

1.

2.

ONE THING I WANT
TO ACCOMPLISH TODAY

1.

DEAR GOD ...

_____

_____

_____

_____

_____

_____

_____

_____

MY CONNECTION TODAY ⟶

day twenty five.

make a date with nature

Access your inner hippie and get connected to nature. Nature has an amazing way of reminding us of the simple pleasures in life. It's also a great way to try those grounding techniques mentioned in the first foundation, Reset emotions.

Maybe you can't escape to the ocean or mountains but you could probably step outside even if it's just to sit on your front porch or to go for a quick walk to the mailbox. Even if you're not a nature lover, try opening your windows to bring in some fresh air or gaze up at the stars. So, we want you to take us on your nature date with you. Well maybe not us, but this book!

Before your nature date:

Where do you plan to go and why?

How are you going to get there?

How long do you hope to stay?

What do you plan to do or not do?

Important: keep your phone on airplane mode (do not disturb) and try to get into nature alone (but be safe!)

After your nature date:

Was where you went, what you expected it to be like?

```


```

Do you think you will go there again? Why or why not?

```


```

What did you do while you were there?

```


```

Was there anything that made your date better than expected?

```


```

Was there anything(s) that made your date worse than expected? If so, what can you change about those things?

```


```

When and where will your next date be?

daily reset

MY OVERALL MOOD: circle one

(poor)   (great)

1   2   3   4   5   6   7   8   9   10

THREE THINGS I'M
THANKFUL FOR

1.

2.

3.

TWO THINGS I'M
EXCITED ABOUT

1.

2.

ONE THING I WANT
TO ACCOMPLISH TODAY

1.

DEAR GOD ...

_____

_____

_____

_____

_____

_____

_____

MY CONNECTION TODAY ⟶

day twenty six.

footloose

How much is music a part of your life? Did you grow up listening to a certain genre or style of music? Maybe you grew up listening to all your parent's favorites and you've grown to love the same groups or maybe you've discovered a new sound just recently that makes you want to dance. Music connects people even when language can't. Sometimes just hearing the first few beats of a song can bring back the sweetest memory.

What do you like most about music? (Circle the ones that best apply and add your own)

The way it makes you feel
How it changes your mood
How it puts words to your thoughts/feelings

_____

_____

_____

Let's turn the page and take it one step further ...

Is the music you listen to uplifting
or bring you down?

What music/songs do you listen to when you want to feel or you do feel...

Happy?

_____

_____

_____

Sad?

_____

_____

_____

Encouraged?

_____

_____

_____

Silly?

_____

_____

_____

Brave?

_____

_____

_____

Read Psalm 105:2. How can you use music to shift you from a place of worry to worship? Pessimism to praise?

_____

_____

_____

daily reset

MY OVERALL MOOD: circle one

(poor)

1   2   3   4   5   6   7   8   9   10   (great)

THREE THINGS I'M
THANKFUL FOR

1.

2.

3.

TWO THINGS I'M
EXCITED ABOUT

1.

2.

ONE THING I WANT
TO ACCOMPLISH TODAY

1.

DEAR GOD ...

_____

_____

_____

_____

_____

_____

_____

MY CONNECTION TODAY ⟶

day twenty seven.

grab a cord, grab a cord next to you.

Maybe it's been tough to find your cord. Finding just one person we can share life with can be difficult, let alone three other people. But, friendship is important so let's not give up. God is relational and he designed us to be in relationships with others, not only to receive love but also to give love.

Qualities and characteristics of a good friend:

Are they trustworthy? (Ways to tell if someone is trustworthy)
- They have their own good, long lasting relationships
- Conversations with them are more encouraging than discouraging
- Gossiping, complaining or criticism are not frequent flyers in your conversations

Are they helpfully honest? (They encourage us to be our best)

Do you admire qualities about them?

Do you have shared interests or are in a similar stage of life?

Are they respectful of your own boundaries?
- Not smothering you with requiring constant interaction
- Honoring/respectful to your family and time you spend with your family

Just as we should be asking these questions about our friends, we should also be asking these questions about ourselves as a friend.!

If you're just venturing out in searching for a friend or you've had friends that have been through the highs and lows with you, think about …

What about them makes you smile?

How do you make them smile?

Plan a cord date (no need to be fancy or feel free to be)

daily reset

MY OVERALL MOOD: circle one

(poor)

1   2   3   4   5   6   7   8   9   10

(great)

THREE THINGS I'M THANKFUL FOR

1.

2.

3.

TWO THINGS I'M EXCITED ABOUT

1.

2.

ONE THING I WANT TO ACCOMPLISH TODAY

1.

DEAR GOD ...

_____

_____

_____

_____

_____

_____

_____

MY CONNECTION TODAY ⟶

day twenty eight.

giving back

One of the best ways to reset emotions, restore thoughts and renew our spirit is to give back. Depression and anxiety can lie to us as we learned in the restore thoughts foundation. The lies can persuade us to isolate and disconnect from the very people and places that can be the most helpful. Not only can we find ourselves removing ourselves from help, we also take ourselves out of the game to help others.

How can you give back...

To your family?

To your friends?

To your church and/or community?

daily reset

MY OVERALL MOOD: circle one

(poor)   (great)

1   2   3   4   5   6   7   8   9   10

THREE THINGS I'M
THANKFUL FOR

1.

2.

3.

TWO THINGS I'M
EXCITED ABOUT

1.

2.

ONE THING I WANT
TO ACCOMPLISH TODAY

1.

DEAR GOD ...

_____

_____

_____

_____

_____

_____

_____

MY CONNECTION TODAY ⟶

day twenty nine.

what's your pattern?

"Do not conform to the pattern of this world, but be transformed by the renewing of your mind. Then you will be able to test and approve what God's will is – his good, pleasing and perfect will." Romans 12:2 (NIV)

Take a few minutes to read and re-read this verse. Circle the words conform, transformed, renewing, and God's will. Those are some powerful words. Conform for example is represents you obeying and imitating a person or lifestyle. Conform is a choice. You are either conforming to the world's culture or to God. Before you answer the following questions, ask God for His wisdom and discernment to know how He wants to use this verse to change your life forever.

What is the "pattern of this world" that God does not want you to conform with?

_____

_____

In what ways have you conformed?

_____

_____

Write down specific thoughts that go on in your mind that you would like renewed.

_____

_____

Being transformed is a continual journey we all are on. As we continue the process of being transformed through a relationship with God, His plan will be revealed. What have you noticed has been transformed in your life through this workbook?

_____

_____

daily reset

MY OVERALL MOOD: circle one

(poor)   (great)

1   2   3   4   5   6   7   8   9   10

THREE THINGS I'M
THANKFUL FOR

1.

2.

3.

TWO THINGS I'M
EXCITED ABOUT

1.

2.

ONE THING I WANT
TO ACCOMPLISH TODAY

1.

DEAR GOD ...

_____

_____

_____

_____

_____

_____

_____

MY CONNECTION TODAY ⟶

day thirty.

foundation recap

time to answer the following questions:

Where did you spend your emotional energy?

_____

Did you learn anything new about yourself?

_____

What new techniques helped you?

_____

What did your journaling reveal to you?

_____

Have you checked in with your Cord recently? Yes or No (If no, text or call them now!)

_____

heart inventory

The Heart Inventory is comprised of 15 questions that will help you better understand how you're doing through this emotional transformation journey. Answer the following questions as you feel today. On a scale from 1-4 with 1 being "Never" and 4 representing "Always", circle the number that represents how you currently feel.

fill in a number: 1= never 4= always

Do you feel hopeful?	①	②	③	④
Do you feel connected to others?	①	②	③	④
Do you feel you are progressing?	①	②	③	④
Do you feel happy?	①	②	③	④
Do you feel in control of your feelings?	①	②	③	④
Do you feel closer to God?	①	②	③	④
Is your positive self-talk increasing?	①	②	③	④
Are you getting enough sleep?	①	②	③	④
Are you exercising regularly?	①	②	③	④
Are you practicing thankfulness?	①	②	③	④
Are you focusing your mind on the present?	①	②	③	④
Do you feel more at peace with self?	①	②	③	④
Are you finding ways to serve others?	①	②	③	④
Are you choosing a positive attitude?	①	②	③	④
Do you have control of your thoughts?	①	②	③	④

Total of all the filled in numbers: _____

If the total to your Heart Inventory is from:

15-29:
This indicates you may be struggling more than feeling encouraged. This is normal and all part of the process! When feeling overwhelmed review The Daily Resets and spend time revisiting the worksheets in this foundation.

30-36:
This indicates that you may be struggling but change is occurring and your hope is increasing! Keep the momentum going and praise God!

37+:
This indicates hope and change are occurring! You are doing it! Keep doing what you are doing because it is working!

daily reset

MY OVERALL MOOD: circle one

(poor)   (great)

1   2   3   4   5   6   7   8   9   10

THREE THINGS I'M
THANKFUL FOR

1.

2.

3.

TWO THINGS I'M
EXCITED ABOUT

1.

2.

ONE THING I WANT
TO ACCOMPLISH TODAY

1.

DEAR GOD ...

_____

_____

_____

_____

_____

_____

_____

MY CONNECTION TODAY ⟶

day thirty one.

launching

Congrats!!! You chose to embark on this journey of emotional transformation, beginning with resetting your emotions, renewing your mind, and restoring your spirit. And we couldn't be more excited or proud of you. If we could, we would reach through these pages and give you a hug. But don't try hugging the book, you may get a paper cut. We want you to know we have prayed for every hand that would reach to pick up these books. We know that this process and journey is not for the faint of heart. To be emotionally transformed is an arduous process but it is a gift that God desires for us. He wants us to renew our mind by knowing who we are. The only way to know who you are is to know whose you are, and you are a child of God. We truly hope you have set aside not only time but also your focus and energy to invest in this journey because you are not only investing in yourself, which is an invaluable gift, you are investing in your legacy and your eternity.

We know that each page offered new challenges and may have increased your questions, but that is the best place to be. There is no end to knowing yourself. Questions come from a heart that is stirred to wonder and to seek after truth. We believe that it was no accident that you found yourself with this workbook in your hands. God wants you to know Him and to know you as He knows you. Knowing who you are and what you're about is more than just knowing your likes and dislikes, or your hopes and fears. Knowing yourself starts with knowing the one who designed you. Knowing that you are beautifully and wonderfully made. You are more complex in the best of ways because the God of the universe created you and he knows your name! Complexity is God's specialty.

Let's keep the momentum going! In order to continue emotional transformation, don't lose sight of why you're doing this. You are on a journey to knowing the greater version of you!

One of the biggest barriers to experiencing emotional transformation is creating long-term success.

Here are some tips for sustainability:
1. **Continue** with The Daily Reset.
2. **Stay connected,** especially with your Cord.
3. **Recycle the pain,** take what you've learned from this journey and share and help others with their own journey.
4. **Revisit your workbook** and review your growth.
5. **Prioritize God** by remaining yoked with Him.

To continue your journey of emotional growth and for more tools, videos and information, visit:

www.theresetgroup.com

We would love to hear from you and how you liked the workbook. Your story inspires us and others. Feel free to DM us through our Instagram @theresetgroup and tell us what you learned about yourself and how you liked the workbook

appendix.

Depression

What are the symptoms of depression?

- Depressed mood or sadness most of the time
- Lack of energy
- Inability to enjoy things that used to bring pleasure
- Withdrawal from friends and family
- Irritability, anger, or anxiety
- Inability to concentrate
- Significant weight loss or gain
- Significant change in sleep patterns (inability to fall asleep, stay asleep, or get up in the morning)
- Feelings of guilt or worthlessness
- Aches and pains (with no known medical cause)
- Pessimism and indifference (not caring about anything in the present or future)
- Thoughts of death or suicide

When someone has five or more of these symptoms more often than not for two weeks or longer, that person is probably depressed.

How is depression different from regular sadness?

Everyone has some ups and downs, and sadness is a natural emotion. The normal stresses of life can lead anyone to feel sad every once in a while. Things like an argument with a friend or spouse, loss of a job, life transitions such as moving or getting a new job or starting a new school, not being chosen for a team, or a best friend moving out of town can lead to feelings of sadness, disappointment, or grief. These reactions are usually brief and go away with a little time and care.

Depression is more than occasionally feeling blue, sad, or down in the dumps, though. Depression is a strong mood involving sadness, discouragement, despair, or hopelessness that lasts for an extended period of time. It interferes with a person's ability to participate in normal activities.

Depression affects a person's thoughts, outlook, and behavior as well as mood. In addition to a depressed mood, a person with depression may feel tired, irritable, and notice changes in appetite. When someone has depression, it can cloud everything. The world looks bleak and the person's thoughts reflect that hopelessness. Depression tends to create negative and self-critical thoughts. Because of feelings of sadness and low energy, those with depression may pull away from those around them or from activities they once enjoyed. This usually makes them feel more lonely and isolated, worsening their condition. Depression can be mild or severe. At its worst, depression can create such feelings of despair that a person contemplates suicide.

Why does someone become depressed?

There is no single cause for depression. Many factors play a role including genetics, life events, family and social environment and medical conditions.

Genetics: Research shows that some individuals inherit genes that make it more likely for them to get depressed. However, not everyone who has the genetic makeup for depression becomes depressed, and many who have no family history of depression have the condition.

Life Events: The death of a family member, friend, or pet can sometimes go beyond normal grief and lead to depression. Other difficult life events, such as when parents divorce, separate, or remarry, can trigger depression. Even events like moving or changing schools can be emotionally challenging enough that a person becomes depressed.

Family and Social Environment: A negative, stressful, or unhappy family atmosphere can have a negative effect on one's self-esteem and lead to depression. This can also include high-stress living situations such as poverty, homelessness, or violence. Substance abuse could cause chemical changes in the brain that negatively impact mood. The damaging social and personal consequences of substance abuse can also lead to depression.

Medical Conditions: Certain medical conditions can affect hormone balance and therefore lead to depression. When these medical conditions are diagnosed and treated by a doctor, the depression usually disappears. For some, undiagnosed learning disabilities might block school, work or relationship success, hormonal changes might affect mood, or physical illnesses might present challenges or setbacks.

How do I get help?

Depression is one of the most common emotional problems around the world. The good news is that it's also one of the most treatable conditions. Those who get help for their depression have a better quality of life and enjoy themselves in ways that they weren't able to before.

Treatment for depression can include psychotherapy, medication, or a combination of both. Psychotherapy with a mental health professional is very effective in treating depression. Therapy sessions can help one understand more about why they feel depressed and learn ways to combat it. Sometimes, doctors prescribe medicine for a patient with depression. It can take a few weeks before that person feels the medicine working. Because every person's brain is different, what works well for one person might not work for another.

Everyone can benefit from mood-boosting activities like exercise, yoga, dance, journaling, or art. It can also help to keep busy no matter how tired you feel.
Those who are depressed shouldn't wait around hoping it will go away on its own; depression can be effectively treated. Others may need to step in if someone seems severely depressed and isn't getting help.

Many find that it helps to open up to others including friends, family or other individuals they trust. Simply saying, "I've been feeling really down lately and I think I'm depressed," can be a good way to begin the discussion. Ask to arrange an appointment with a therapist. For teens, if a parent or family member can't help, turn to a school counselor, best friend, or a helpline.

Anxiety

Introduction to Anxiety

Generalized Anxiety Disorder or GAD is characterized by excessive, exaggerated anxiety about everyday life events. People with symptoms of GAD tend to always expect disaster and can't stop worrying about health, money, family, work, or school. These worries are often unrealistic or out of proportion for the situation. Daily life becomes a constant state of unease, fear, and dread. Eventually, the anxiety so dominates the person's thinking that it interferes with daily functioning.

What is anxiety?

Anxiety is a natural human reaction that serves an important basic survival function. It acts as an alarm system that is activated whenever a person perceives danger. When the body reacts to a potential threat, a person feels physical sensations of anxiety: a faster heartbeat and breath rate, tensed muscles, sweaty palms, nausea, and trembling hands or legs. These sensations are part of the body's fight-flight response, which is caused by a rush of adrenaline and other chemicals. This reaction prepares the body to make a quick decision to either stay and fight that threat or try to escape from it (fight or flight). It takes a few seconds longer for the thinking part of the brain (the cortex) to process the situation and evaluate whether the threat is real, and if it is, how to handle it. If the cortex sends the all-clear signal, the fight-flight response is deactivated and the nervous system can relax. If the brain reasons that a threat might last, feelings of anxiety and the physical symptoms listed above may linger, keeping the person alert.

What are the symptoms of Generalized Anxiety Disorder?

Generalized Anxiety Disorder (GAD) affects the way a person thinks, but the anxiety can lead to physical symptoms as well. Symptoms of GAD include:

- Excessive, ongoing worry and tension
- An unrealistic view of problems
- Restlessness or a feeling of being "edgy"

- Irritability
- Muscle tension
- Headaches
- Sweating
- Difficulty concentrating
- Nausea
- The need to go to the bathroom frequently
- Tiredness
- Trouble falling or staying asleep
- Trembling
- Being easily startled
- Other anxiety disorders (panic disorder, obsessive-compulsive disorder, phobias, etc.)
- Depression
- Drug/alcohol abuse

What causes Geralized Anxiety Disorder?

Although the exact cause of GAD is not known, a number of factors, including genetics, brain chemistry, and environmental stressors appear to contribute to its development.
Genetics: Some research suggests that family history plays a part in increasing the likelihood that a person will develop GAD. This means that the tendency to develop GAD may be passed on in families.

Brain chemistry: GAD has been associated with abnormal levels of certain neurotransmitters in the brain. Neurotransmitters are special chemical messengers that help move information between nerve cells. If the neurotransmitters are out of balance, messages cannot travel through the brain properly. This can alter the way the brain reacts in certain situations, leading to anxiety.

Environmental factors: Trauma and stressful events, such as abuse, the death of a loved one, divorce, or changing jobs or schools may lead to GAD. The use of and withdrawal from addictive substances, including alcohol, caffeine, and nicotine, could also worsen anxiety.

How are anxiety disorders treated?

Anxiety disorders can be treated by both mental health professionals and therapists. A therapist can look at the symptoms someone is dealing with, diagnose the specific anxiety disorder, and create a plan to help the person get relief. A particular type of talk therapy called cognitive-behavior therapy (CBT) is often used. In CBT, a person learns new ways to think and act in situations that can cause anxiety, and to manage and deal with stress. The therapist provides support and guidance and teaches new coping skills such as relaxation techniques or breathing exercises. Sometimes, but not always, medication is used as part of the treatment for anxiety.

How common is Generalized Anxiety Disorder?

About 4 million American adults suffer from GAD during the course of a year. It most often begins in childhood or adolescence, but can begin in adulthood. It is more common in women than in men.

How to Win the Night

Our go-to's if you are struggling to fall asleep or stay asleep:

Setting yourself up for a good night's rest:
- Create a nightly routine (taking a shower or bath, put on soft music, dim the lights).
- Start the process of preparing for sleep an hour before.
- Go to bed the same time every night.
- Turn off all electronics and/or put the phone face down.

Trouble falling asleep or going back to sleep:
- Reflect on your blessings and what you are grateful for.
- Count backwards from 100.
- Have a notepad next to your bed to write down any pending to do's or thoughts.
- Relax your body by telling your body to go to sleep, starting with your toes and going up to your head.
- After 30 minutes of not being able to fall asleep, get up and do something and then return to your bed.

Treatment for Self Mutilators

A number of different treatment approaches are used with self-mutilators, including psychodynamic psychotherapy, group therapy, journaling, and behavioral therapy.

Persons who mutilate themselves should seek treatment from a depth-psychodynamic therapist for their hurts/pain and a therapist who is knowledgeable in cognitive-behavioral therapy to help with healthy coping skills. Most self-mutilators are treated as outpatients, although there are some inpatient programs for adolescent females. Only six percent of self-mutilators commit suicide. Most self-mutilators are not suicidal; they are hurting on the inside from past pain that keeps controlling their lives.

Remember, self-mutilation is primarily a means of releasing tension, trying to express your emotions in a physical way, communicating, or reliving painful experiences. Although there are no medications specifically for self-mutilation, antidepressants are often given, particularly if the patient meets the diagnostic criteria for a depressive disorder. The following are recommended for treatment:

- All treatment plans for self mutilators need the following: Active listening/validating/empathy
- Art therapy: Art therapy is used to help the teenager express themselves in a healthy way. Color and shading is very important to be aware of on their drawings. Look for common themes and ask the client to tell a story about their art. Keep the art over time as away to measure how far the client has gone in therapy.
- Music: Have the client bring in their music that reminds them of the pain they are feeling when they want to mutilate themselves. Moreover have them bring music that reminds them of how they want to feel. Make a CD of the music so they can use it in time of pain. Guitars, keyboards, and drums can be used in therapy to help them express their pain and fight the resistance that might be there.
- Exercise: Working out can be used as a coping mechanism or a safe outlet for anger.
- Psychiatric care: Studies show that psychiatric care at times can be detrimental to the client. Most cases of self-mutilators, the issue isn't a chemical lacking in the brain, but a cry for help! They want a safe empathetic environment where they can express their pain to someone who cares. For example, usually in the case of a cutter there is absolutely nothing wrong with the cutters brain, no evidence of any kind of bio-chemical cause for the depression, and therefore the chemicals do more harm than good and are an inappropriate form of treatment.

- Insight: Help the client to understand the environmental triggers that causes the pain that leads to the self-mutilation.

Too often, care providers/therapists focus on stopping the mutilating (cutting, burning, etc.) as quickly as possible because they themselves are not comfortable with it, it repulses them, makes them feel ineffective, frightens them, etc. Situations like this can easily deteriorate into a power struggle in which the therapist insists that the behavior stop and the client chooses to self-injure covertly and becomes reticent and distrustful, thus reducing the chance that a useful therapeutic alliance will be formed. The behavior itself will not be fixed right away. At times it can take months before the client has the insight of why they are cutting. The therapist needs to concentrate on the underlying issues and not the symptoms/behaviors that the pain is causing.

An ideal approach would be one in which clients mutilations is tolerated but has specific consequences. For example, a client might be invited to contact the therapist when an urge to self-harm occurs, but restricted from contact for 24 hours after an actual self-injurious act. In a system like this, the self-injurer has a chance to articulate what she/he is trying to communicate through her/his body without having to resort to self-injury, and she/he knows that carrying through an act of mutilations will have tangible and immediate (but not permanent) negative effects. This kind of agreement between therapist and client can help stabilize the mutilation and clear the road for dealing with the issues underlying the need to injure. This allows the therapist to treat self-harm within the context of underlying pathology without making the cutting behavior the main focus.

Patients must have the following to be successful in therapy:

- must have a heartfelt motivation to stop
- have the right to voluntarily stop therapy at any time
- must sign a "no-self-harm contract" before starting therapy
- are discouraged from exhibiting or discussing scars with anyone to prevent contagion
- must refer to their behavior as self-injury
- must complete all homework assignments that focus on the negative consequences of self-injury and the benefits of staying free of self-harm
- are expected to develop and practice at least five alternatives to self mutilation

Suicide Ideation

If you are having suicidal thoughts connect with someone as soon as possible, whether that be a professional, a family member, a friend, or a significant other. Tell them what you are thinking and feeling. Call the suicide hotline 1-800-784-2433 for additional support. For the next 24 hours do not be alone. If you have thoughts, a plan, and means of harming yourself dial 911 or go to your local hospital immediately.

Panic/Anxiety Attack

Choose one or all of the following, whatever works best for you:

Squeeze ice or hold a cold drink.

IMPORTANCE: This cools down your CNS (Central Nervous System) and redirects your thoughts onto the coldness of the ice instead of focusing on your anxious thoughts

Breathe in through your nose and blow out through your mouth.
Pierce your lips to maximize your oxygen levels.

IMPORTANCE: Your lungs trap oxygen during the time of an attack and this helps you get your oxygen out while at the same time maximizing the oxygen levels in your body.

Get outside. Go for a walk and as you walk shift your eyes from left to right.

IMPORTANCE: This gets your body moving and back in control of your body. Fresh air is a good change of environment. When you move your eyes from left to right it brings tranquility to the brain.

Repeat this phrase: Say the following mantra over and over again: "God is in control, I am okay. I am okay, God is in control."

IMPORTANCE: This gets your mind focused off yourself and gives you positive self-talk.

Practice grounding exercises using your five senses. What do you hear, see, smell, taste, or feel around you?

IMPORTANCE: Activating your five senses will help bring you into the here and now.

Coping Skills and Defense Mechanisms

Defense Mechanisms: Unhealthy ways we respond to our thoughts and emotions.

Coping Skills: Healthy ways we respond to our thoughts and emotions.

Defense Mechanisms:

- Avoiding responsibilities
- Blaming others
- Denial of problems
- Catastrophizing problems
- Displacement-transferring emotions onto other innocent things or people
- Day dreaming
- Acting out/Throwing a tantrum
- Become controlling
- Repression
- Yelling
- Projecting
- Cutting
- Over/Under eating
- Over sleeping
- Substance abuse
- Sarcasm/Humor
- Regression
- Passive Aggressiveness
- Victimization
- Comparison
- Going shopping

Coping Skills:

- Deep breathing
- Positive Self-Talk
- "Stinkin' Thinkin'" worksheet
- Sharing your need
- Exercising
- Journaling
- Drawing
- Listen to music
- Squeeze ice
- Pray
- Write what you are thankful for
- Read scriptures
- Take a bath or shower
- Interact with your pet (if applicable)
- Eat a healthy snack
- Go for a drive
- Read a book
- Do a puzzle
- Write, draw, paint, photography
- Play an instrument, sing, dance, act
- Do some gardening
- Watch a good movie
- Play a board/card game
- Clean or organize your environment
- Lower your expectations of the situation
- Keep an inspirational quote with you
- Scream in a pillow
- Punch a pillow
- Cry
- Laugh

joy healers & stealers.

joy healers (growth mindset)	joy stealers (fixed mindset)
Focus your MIND not on how it is, but how it can be and SHOULD be.	Inward CRITIQUING of self.
Learn how to CELEBRATE others.	Outward COMPLAINING of others or your current situation.
Be GRATEFUL and live in the PRESENT.	SOCIAL MEDIA and disconnection of the present.
Be POSITIVE and ask for ACCOUNTABILITY.	Being RESULT or outcome driven.

mindset map of positivity

	MANUFACTURED BY	DRIVEN BY	FOCUS ON
Joy	Internal Choice	Relationship with self	How it can be and should be
Happy	Situational Driven	Relationship with environment	The present & here and now
Fun	Dynamic between two people or more	Relationship with others	In-Person connection with others.

10 SCIENTIFIC WAYS TO BE HAPPY

PRAY
REWRITE YOUR BRAIN

SPEND TIME WITH FAMILY & FRIENDS

PRACTICE SMILING

START
DON'T PROCRASTINATE

PLAN AN ACTIVITY

GO OUTSIDE

HELP OTHERS
2 HOURS A WEEK

GET MORE SLEEP

PRACTICE GRATITUDE

EXERCISE
AT LEAST 7 MINUTES A DAY

RESET
PERFORMANCE MINDSET COACHING

6 BAD HABITS
THAT DRAIN
YOUR ENERGY

ALWAYS ON
SOCIAL
MEDIA

LIVING
IN THE
PAST

STAYING
AROUND
NEGATIVITY

REGULARLY
OVERTHINKING

STAYING UP
LATE

CONSTANT
UNHEALTHY
EATING

www.theresetgroup.com

151

about the authors

joe & kristin jardine

Some may call Kristin and Joe competitive card players, others may call them foodies, as they love trying new restaurants. You can usually find Joe and Kristin spending time with their two kids, family and friends or slicing a ball out on the tennis court.

Joe, not only sees clients at his local private practice offices, he is the founder of The Reset Group where he works as a performance mindset coach with NFL quarterbacks and coaches, and college football teams. He is also an adolescent psychology professor at Vanguard University and is a keynote speaker at youth camps and conferences around California.

Kristin Jardine is an actress turned speaker. While she still works in the entertainment industry as a voice over artist, she has a passion for speaking and telling her story to help encourage others. She speaks at woman conferences, MOPS/mom groups and youth camps around CA.

daniel & rennié simpson

Daniel and Rennié Simpson are both Licensed Marriage & Family Therapists. Through private practice, they help individuals, couples, families and teens to learn practical and sustainable ways to improve how they see themselves, their relationships and their future. In life, we're either moving towards flourishing or away from it and Daniel and Rennié want everyone to know and live a life that is flourishing. They enjoy speaking together at conferences, workshops and even their local coffee shop, to share ways to live with intention.

If you'd like to contact them or grab a coffee, Daniel & Rennié can be found at www.youflourishing.com

Made in the USA
Las Vegas, NV
16 October 2022

57419290R10090